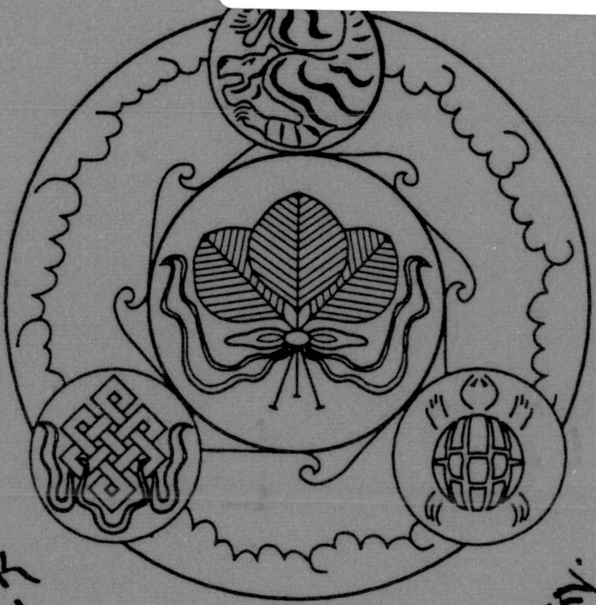

ཆོས་ཀྱི་རྒྱལ་མཚན་ལེགས་པར་འཛུགས་

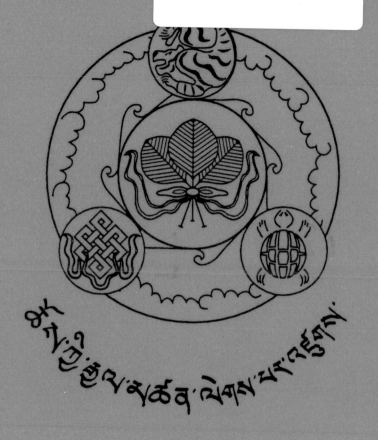

ཀ༌ལཱ༔བ༌ཀ༷ཙ༔བརྙན༷ཅ༷ཙ༷ག༷ཅ༷ཙ༔ཆ༔ཀ༷ཙ༔ཆ༷ལཱ

ༀ། རང་གི་བླ་ཆེན་སྤྲུལ་སྐུ་པ་བྱམས་པ་མཐའ་ཡས་ཀྱིས་གསར་དུ་
བརྩམས་གནང་མཛད་པའི་ཁྲིད་ཡིག་འདིས་ ༈ སྟོན་པ་བླ་ན་མེད་པའི་གསུང་
གི་སྙིང་པོ་སྒོམ་གྱི་སྒོར་ལ་ ཁ་མས་ཞིན་ཤེད་འདུན་ཡོད་པའི་བསོད་ནམས་ཕུན་སུམ་
ཚོགས་པ་ཅན་རྣམས་ལ་ ཕན་པ་རྒྱ་ཆེན་པོ་འབྱུང་ངེས་པས་ དཔལ་ལྡན་དགེ་
བའི་རྒྱལ་ཁབ་ཆེན་པོ་དངྒྲ་ཡུལ་གྱིས་གཙོ་བོར་གྱུར་པའི་ཡངས་པའི་རྒྱལ་ཁམས་རྣམས་
ཀྱི་དམ་པའི་ཆོས་ལ་དད་ལྡན་ཐམས་ཅད་ཀྱིས་བློ་སྦྱོང་བྱེད་རྒྱག་ལ་ཆེ་བ་ཡིན་ནོ། ཞེས་
པ་འང་ འཕགས་པ་སྤྱན་རས་གཟིགས་ཀྱི་འདུལ་ཞིང་ དམ་པ་ཆོས་ཀྱི་འབྱུང་གནས་
བོད་ཡུལ་གྱི་སྐྱ་མི་རྐངས་པོ་ ཀརྨ་ཕྲིན་ལས་པས་ རབ་བྱུང་བཅུ་བདུན་པ་ དགའ་བྱེད་
མཁའ་འགྲོ་རྒྱལ་མོའི་ལོ་ལ་བྲིས་པ་དགེ་ལེགས་འཕེལ།

This guide, recently composed by my regent Ngakpa Jampa Thaye, will be very beneficial to those meritorious people who aspire to practise meditation, the essence of the peerless Teacher's instructions. Therefore it is important that all who have faith in dharma whether in England or elsewhere should study this.

Thus was written by Karma Thinleypa from Tibet the source of the holy dharma and the field of conversion of Arya Avalokitesvara, in the year of the Garuda Queen in the seventeenth Rab-jung cycle (January 1994). May virtue and goodness increase.

First published in Great Britain in 1994.

ISBN 0 9509119 5X

British Library cataloguing and publication data. The cataloguing record
for this book is available from British Library.

GANESHA PRESS
27 Lilymead Avenue
Bristol

Thangka painting by Rana Lister
Design and Typesetting by Pen to Paper Design Group

Leap
like a
Tiger

Walk
like a
Tortoise

Introduction

T his book is for people who are interested in learning about Buddhist meditation. The author, Jampa Thaye (David Stott), has trained under the Tibetan meditation master Karma Thinley Rinpoche for over twenty years and has been authorised by his teacher to transmit to others the teachings he has received and practised.

There are many books on Buddhism, many books on meditation. Yet it still remains hard to find a book that sets out clearly and unmistakably the essentials of Buddhist meditation practice. Moreover, when so many different books are available, how can we be sure of each one's relevance to our needs or even its reliability? The value of Jampa Thaye's book lies in the fact that it springs directly from the experience of a Western person who has studied and put into practice the authentic Buddhist teachings and through them attained true spiritual realisation.

The book itself follows a pattern which to some extent mirrors what happens when we first come into contact with meditation and begin to practise it. To start with, we want to have some simple introductory explanation, some brief overview of what Buddhist meditation involves. Then we like to have an opportunity to ask questions, to air our concerns and uncertainties and to look at them afresh from the perspective of meditation. Eventually we may feel that we want to find out more about meditation and the nature of mind and that we are ready to begin exploring the teachings in greater depth and detail.

The three sections of the book correspond to these three stages. In the first part, *Leap Like a Tiger, Walk Like a Tortoise*, Jampa Thaye introduces us to Buddhist meditation and explains the key elements of the spiritual path. In the second part, *Questions Asked, Answers Given,* he answers many of the fundamental questions that people raise when they begin to meditate. *Heart of Gold*, the third and final section of the book, focuses on the nature of mind and shows us how by following the stages of the Buddhist path we can uncover the natural purity of our mind.

Leap Like a Tiger, Walk Like a Tortoise has been conceived out of the need for a clear and concise introduction to Buddhist practice. Many people who are interested in learning about meditation or who have already embarked on the path have requested such a book. Jampa Thaye has kindly responded to their request with this collection of teachings. On behalf of everyone, I would like to take this opportunity to thank Jampa Thaye. Thanks are also due to Kenneth Houston and Isabel Glasow, who helped with the preparation of the text, and to Nigel Harper and Richard Ryan, who supervised the book's production.

A word of warning! Nowhere in these pages will the reader find the mixed-up confusion of blind assertions and borrowed techniques that too often passes for spiritual instruction nowadays. Jampa Thaye, like his teacher Karma Thinley Rinpoche, remains true to the uncompromising vision of the Buddhist tradition. This vision is of a mind freed from delusion and suffering, with the power to truly benefit all other beings. Delusion and suffering are no different now than they were when Buddha first showed the way to liberation. The key qualities of the Buddhist path, wisdom and compassion, are real qualities; rooted firmly in the erosion of our deluded self-clinging, ripening into the timeless wisdom that sees the true nature of reality and the limitless compassion that embraces all living beings.

There is nothing mysterious about meditation. It is supremely practical: a way to enable us to experience things as they truly are. Buddha's teachings are not arcane or academic. They are not meant to be mummified in libraries and museums - they are meant to be lived. In this book Jampa Thaye shows us how we can live them.

Geoffrey Ashmore
January 1994

The Tiger And The Tortoise
First steps in Meditation

I n Tibet there is a saying that the way to approach meditation is first of all to leap like a tiger and then secondly to walk like a tortoise. What this means is that if we want to practise meditation we first need to get an overall view of the teachings very rapidly: then, when we have gained that initial view of the path, we can go back and start again at the beginning, covering the same ground slowly and systematically, understanding each step properly. First leap like a tiger, then walk like a tortoise.

These days it is more important than ever to have this overall view, because Buddha's teachings are so new to people living in the West. There are many names and ideas which are unfamiliar and the teachings themselves are so vast that it is easy to become lost in complexity, especially at the beginning. There is a danger that we might take just a little bit of the teachings and think this is the essence of Buddhism or even the whole of it.

But in doing this we might be like the blindfolded men who are set to examine a certain animal. Each one takes hold of a different part of the creature, so that one of them thinks it is a rhinoceros, another thinks it is a horse and so on. But when the blindfolds are removed, they see that in fact the animal is an elephant. The situation is similar with meditation. When we approach it for the first time, unless we are given a view of the whole thing, it is easy to get mistaken ideas about it by taking just one part and ignoring the rest. Therefore it is very good to have an introduction to the fundamental basis of the spiritual path. Then we can move on and follow the path systematically.

VIEW, MEDITATION, ACTION

The Buddhist path is often described in terms of three key elements: view, meditation and action. Each of these is interconnected.

To understand the view is to understand the true nature of things. When we understand this, we can successfully meditate and become one with the true nature of reality. But we do not really understand the view unless we start to do meditation practice. Without meditation practice our understanding of Buddha's teachings on the true nature of the world is purely intellectual. Similarly, if we meditate but do not put these teachings into practice in our everyday lives - learning how to cherish others with compassion - then the teachings are useless. They are wasted.

VIEW

Everybody has a 'view', a way of seeing. We all have different ways of seeing and, depending on the way we see the world, we act and behave in a certain way; we have certain roles and ambitions, certain things we are trying to achieve. But Buddha said that actually most of our ways of perceiving the world are mistaken. We do not see things as they truly are.

The fundamental mistake is the belief in a real solid entity which is ourselves and a real solid world which is external to ourselves. These ideas are actually make believe. There is no such solid, unchangeable entity inside ourselves and there is no solid, unchanging, dependable world outside. We have grown used to the idea that such things exist. We devoutly believe that these things exist - but they do not.

This is called 'the lion's roar of reason': the announcement that there really isn't any solid self inside of us or external to us. And it is this that is the hallmark of all Buddha's teachings, the characteristic that differentiates Buddhist teachings (the dharma) from other philosophies.

To understand this central aspect of Buddha's teachings, we must receive a great deal of instruction, listen to and study many presentations of the dharma and then really analyse it for ourselves until we become convinced of its validity. When we have done that, then we can meditate and make our understanding an actual lived experience: so that right in our hearts we see there are no solid entities, either inside or outside. This is the Buddhist vision: the view of non-self.

A further, deeper way of expressing this vision was communicated by the Buddha when he taught that, although there is no solid existing self inside or outside ourselves, the true nature of our mind is buddha nature.

Up to this point in time we have not recognised our buddha nature. But if we turn inwards and look directly into our mind, we will see that it is completely open, completely luminous, clear and unobstructed. It has no beginning, no end, no dwelling place - and yet it is the basis for all appearances. This ungraspable, ineffable nature of mind is what is called buddha nature and it is the true core of every being's awareness. All beings from the smallest to the greatest possess this buddha nature, which is the fundamental original state of being.

But we have forgotten this. The original, true nature of our mind has become obscured by our forgetfulness and all the mistaken ideas which have arisen as a result of that forgetfulness. Our unawareness or ignorance has led us to believe that our bodies, our thoughts, our emotions are solid, permanent and unchanging and that around us there are solid, unchanging, separate objects. But all these are just fantasies or dreams, mistaken ways of seeing things.

Beneath our confusion, however, the true nature of awareness is unchanging and unaltered. Our original awareness, our buddha nature, remains open, clear and unobstructed. And when we are introduced to that, then we are really introduced to the view.

MEDITATION

The view shows us what is real, what is true. But to understand the view is not in itself sufficient: we must experience buddha nature for ourselves. And we do that through meditation.

Normally when people talk about meditation they talk about qualities such as calmness, stillness, becoming more at ease. All these qualities are truly good qualities of meditation but the essence of meditation, the gift of meditation, is to settle into buddha nature, to relax in this primordial reality. There is no other thing for us to do. Once we have received instructions on the view of meditation, then we must experience it for ourselves.

This is the deepest form of meditation. And as such, it does not consist of trying to produce or manufacture something - not even a state of calmness or wisdom. All we need to do is simply to relax and to allow what is already there, our buddha nature, to manifest.

This is the true key point of meditation. In order to actualise our understanding of our own buddha nature, in order to know it for ourselves, we must relax in meditation.

ACTION

As we learn to relax in buddha nature through our meditation, so our way of dealing with the world, with people and situations, begins to change. We find that we can act and respond to things in an unforced and spontaneous way. This way of acting arises naturally from our meditation.

Generally in Buddhism when we are considering actions, we examine the things we do and see the extent to which they are selfish and indulgent or even abusive of others. Then we try to change the way we act and to develop better, more morally wholesome kinds of behaviour. In the end, however, this is only a superficial way of acting. The deepest kind of action is the one that arises naturally.

The more we can relax in the true nature of mind, the more our actions will issue directly from our heart, untouched by self - centeredness. And in this way our actions become truly compassionate, because they come directly out of the space of non-self. Sometimes this is called bodhisattva activity. The bodhisattva is the compassionate being whose activity arises spontaneously.

View, meditation and action: these three are the core of the Buddhist path. There may be different Buddhist teachings, many different books written by the masters of the various lineages; there may be many different rituals and many different meditation practices but all of them converge on these three points: the view of buddha nature, the meditation in which we rest in this natural state and the effortless, compassionate activity which arises from our realisation. These three together are like the nectar of all the thousands of Dharma teachings.

BOTH EYES OPEN

We need two eyes to see the world around us and in Dharma too this seems to be necessary. We need to approach our meditation practice with both eyes open . To use the analogy of the tiger and the tortoise again in a slightly different way, we could say that we need to have one tiger's eye and one tortoise's eye. With the tortoise's eye we can see that if we are to change we need to follow the discipline of the spiritual path and train properly, for example by developing positive moral behaviour. But to think that mere observance of the correct behaviour will produce inner realisation is a one-sided and mistaken viewpoint. With the tiger's eye we need to see that real morality, real compassion, is not created by following any discipline at all but is what comes naturally out of an open, awakened heart.

If we see with both these eyes, then we have a balanced view. We can see that true compassion is completely spontaneous and that moral discipline is only a skilful means to an end. In our present situation, because of our habitual self-indulgence, we need to follow some discipline; but we should do so knowing that the essence of what we are working towards is beyond discipline. It is essential that we have this dual perspective.

We also have to have a clear understanding of each perspective. When we talk about spontaneous activity, for instance, we have to be sure that we understand what we mean by that. The kind of spontaneity we are talking about in dharma is that which arises from a great clarity, a great openness and a great calmness. By contrast, what we often take to be spontaneity in ourselves and others is completely the opposite. It may be no more than saying the first thing that comes into our head or discharging something which is painful to us, getting something off our chest. None of this is very likely to be helpful to the person to whom it is said. We are simply not in tune with the other person. Rather, we are acting in response to our own impulses, following our own agenda. We could call this kind of unthinking activity 'egocentric spontaneity'.

True spontaneity is entirely different from this. It arises in fact from the death of egocentric activity.

Seeing true spontaneity and its source in our own liberated buddha nature is the tiger's vision. We need also, however, to have the tortoise's view and the key quality here is mindfulness. Mindfulness means bringing our mind into the present, recognising where we are and what we are doing. It is focusing on the present moment, on whatever is arising.

Not that mindfulness is just a narrow beam of light. It is also panoramic. It does not focus exclusively on one thing or one action but takes in what is around. It is sensitive to the environment and to the beings in one's environment. Mindfulness is very powerful and dynamic: it acts as a sword, cutting out a great deal of mental rubbish and poison which previously would have caused us to act in an egocentric way.

At the beginning of the spiritual path, the 'walk like a tortoise stage' so to speak, we need to develop some control over ourselves. We need to learn about the quality of moral actions. That is why Buddha prescribed the ten virtuous actions and the five moral precepts (refraining from taking life, from stealing, from sexual misconduct, from false and harmful speech and from intoxication), because by taking on such a discipline we learn to develop qualities beyond discipline itself.

The discipline of not harming, not stealing and so on helps us at first to cut off our ingrained tendency to grab at things, to harm other beings or to blurt out whatever comes into our mind. Discipline acts like a stake which is set in the ground and tied to a young sapling. In order to grow straight, the sapling needs the support of the stake. Learning moral discipline is like that stake. At first the following of moral precepts and the practice of mindfulness are crucial: without them we will never experience any true spiritual growth. Later on the stake can be taken away from the tree, which will now grow straight on its own. Real compassionate action is like the tree when it is grown.

So it is essential that we have these two perspectives: the perspective of self-restraint and the perspective of spontaneity. If we lose sight of one or other perspective, we find ourselves falling into extremes. Either we become too tight in the way we practise, too bound up with technicalities; or else we falsely claim to be enlightened and compassionate and therefore think we have no need to bother with moral precepts. Avoiding these two extremes by maintaining both the vision of the tiger and of the tortoise is what keeps our meditation practice fruitful and balanced.

Meditation

Q Why is meditation important?

A Most of our problems in life stem from the fact that we are not really grounded in the present moment. Our minds are agitated and so we don't have a clear vision of what's happening internally or externally. To achieve this clarity of mind, a clarity that leads ultimately to wisdom, we need to practise meditation. In meditation we allow ourselves to remain in the present moment - both relaxed and attentive. In this state we connect with our natural awareness, which lies beneath the surface of moving thoughts and emotions and is the source of true wisdom and compassion.

Q Is position important and the length of time we meditate for?

A The position is important in meditation in that it creates the right environment for practice. The traditional posture, sitting in the vajra-position, is especially helpful because it brings all the energy currents in our body into a state of harmony particularly conducive to meditation. However, if we can't manage such a posture it is still satisfactory to simply sit in a relaxed way, even in a chair, as long as one's back is straight, though not tense, one's hands are placed together and so on.

As for length of time, there's a saying that beginners should meditate frequently but for quite brief sessions. In other words, one should establish a routine of meditating each day or even twice a day but in order not to strain the mind one should meditate at first for no more than fifteen or twenty minutes. If one attempts too much at first one will tether the mind and induce a kind of artificial concentration when what is necessary is simply to remain in the natural state of awareness.

Q **Do we have to suppress our thoughts and feelings in order to meditate?**

A True meditation is not about suppressing or creating. It is actually a natural state itself. That is all. Nothing added, nothing taken away. Meditation is not something we can bring about by removing something that is already there or by creating something that is not yet there.

If we become tense during meditation because we are suppressing our feelings, it is a sign that our meditation is in fact too tight. We need to relax a little.

Buddha said that getting the right balance in meditation is like tuning a musical instrument. If the string is too slack, it cannot be played; if it is too tight, the string will snap. Similarly if we tighten our mind in meditation, if we try to repress our thoughts and emotions, then we become tense. If we feel that things are being suppressed, then it is time to open up, to relax our mind. On the other hand, if we find our attention wandering away in all kinds of thoughts and fantasies, this is a sign that our meditation is too loose. Our mind is drifting all over the place, so we need to focus our attention and bring it back to the present moment.

It is a question of maintaining a balance: meditation is concentrated but at the same time wide open.

Q **How will we know when we are meditating correctly?**

A With authentic meditation comes a developing sense of ease and spaciousness in our dealings with the world. Things that previously seemed to overwhelm us now appear in a new perspective, so that we can see perhaps for the first time their actual nature. At the same time, our insecurity which has always driven us to focus on our own needs at the expense of others starts to lessen. We become more responsive to the situation of others - a sense of warmth towards them arises.

Conversely one can say that if one's fixations increase and one develops a coldness to others then one's meditation is not proceeding along genuine lines.

Q **When you work and have a family it is very hard to meditate. How is it possible to combine the two?**

A One of the keys to success in meditation practice is to establish a routine. So if one has a family and work responsibilities, one can fairly easily establish times for practice and study that don't conflict with but support these responsibilities. The most obvious point is that one should rise early and accomplish one's principal meditation practice then. Actually it needs to be pointed out that in the usual monastic situation monks and nuns have really no extra time for meditation since they have all their monastic duties to fulfil. They too have to find a private time and space for meditation just like lay-people.

Furthermore, in having a responsibility for a family one is provided with an opportunity to develop the qualities of love and compassion, which can then be extended outwards towards the world family. Also it is well-known that the Buddha taught the Vajrayana specifically to provide means by which we could transform any life-situation, including family and work, into an aspect of the spiritual path. So, all in all, I would say that there is no doubt that we can meditate and follow the spiritual path in the midst of family and work responsibilities.

Q **Why do we have to use meditation within the confines of religion?**

A From the Buddhist point of view the practice of meditation is, so to speak, the engine of the car that leads to complete enlightenment

- a state transcending birth and death. Obviously there are incidental benefits of meditation practice which arise relatively quickly such as feelings of calmness and peace and there's nothing wrong with such things. However, if we attempt to detach meditation from the spiritual path we will see such sensations as ends in themselves and become trapped in attachment to temporary mental phenomena. That will be like taking the engine out of the car to warm our hands on it rather than leaving it in the car so that it can take us to enlightenment. Nowadays many people talk about meditation in this way but it is an entirely different kind of practice to that of Buddhist meditation.

Compassion

Q Westerners often have a view of Buddhism as some kind of way of life that is rather world-denying and introverted.

A Well, I think that is a mistaken view because such people haven't really had the chance to see the full extent of Buddha's teachings. It is true that Lord Buddha said that we have to free ourselves from attachment to worldly objects because such attachment to things that are ultimately impermanent only brings about suffering. However it is actually detachment which allows us the space and breadth of mind to develop more love and compassion for others, because we cannot treat ourselves as self-enclosed entities if we are as dependent on others as they are on us. We are, in other words, all interconnected and interdependent and detachment gives the necessary freedom for compassion, which is the deepest of all motivations for practising dharma. So, while we are free from compulsory attachment, we do have to cherish every being that we encounter, because just as we cherish our own lives and place such a high priority on our own happiness so does every being and we must extend to others the same cherishing that we previously extended to ourselves. Therefore if denying the world means denying beings, that is not the Buddhist way. The Buddhist way is to actually see the illusory nature of all phenomena while avoiding the trap of thinking that we can escape into our own private salvation. Buddha himself spent all his time after he achieved enlightenment making the way of liberation available to others and this is the example we should emulate. Buddha did not cut himself off from the world and neither should we. Therefore detachment, yes, but detachment in order to be able to cherish others without any self-interest, without any bias towards one's own benefit. This is the central ethic of dharma.

Q How do I develop a more compassionate attitude?

A The key to developing a more compassionate attitude is to develop a feeling of our connectedness with others. We can only continue to privilege ourselves at the expense of others as long as we ignore the kinship that exists between ourselves and others. We are, after all, 'limbs of one life'. One particularly helpful way to 'tune in' to this interconnectedness is to see others as our parents or as our children, because obviously such a family situation is the most tangible manifestation of connectedness. Now we wish to be happy and to be free from sorrow but so do all members of our family. How can our wish be more important than theirs? It makes complete sense logically and emotionally to wish them to have the same happiness we wish for ourselves. Then considering that everybody is ultimately part of our world family, we can extend the same love and compassion to them.

Q Which do we start with, meditation or compassion?

A This is rather like asking which comes first, the chicken or the egg! Meditation and compassion cannot be separated. The more compassionate you become, the more you think of others and the less you have time for yourself - so the more your egocentric behaviour lessens. And it is from this, the death of egocentricity, that truly spontaneous meditation arises.

Correspondingly, as your meditation grows stronger and more stable, the more your egocentric behaviour lessens and the more time and space you have for others - so the more compassionate you are! Ultimately meditation and compassion are not two separate things. The more spacious and open you are, the more compassionate you are. The more compassionate you are, the more spacious and open you are. Meditation and compassion work together; we cannot really say that one goes first and the other follows. They help each other.

What is compassion? It is openness: openness to other beings and their sufferings. Everybody has experienced moments of great spontaneity which have been triggered by compassion for others. You see your child in a situation of distress: at that moment your only thought is for that child; there is no room for yourself. The moment will pass and you may well return to your normal, self-involved state but the moment of spontaneous selflessness has happened. Everybody has the capacity for this.

Compassion is inseparable from meditation and in view of this the person who wants to practise meditation should be extremely grateful to others, since they will help us on the path of enlightenment. It is said in the Buddhist teachings that we are just as indebted to other beings for helping us to become enlightened as we are to the Buddhas for teaching us the methods to achieve enlightenment. It is only because there are other sentient beings to trigger off this self-forgetting in us that we can approach enlightenment. So we should never think we are doing some other person a favour by being compassionate - exactly the opposite!

The Teacher

Q Is it always necessary to have a personal teacher?

A If we really want to learn meditation, then we need to have a teacher. This is something that is stressed again and again in the Buddhist teachings. The reason we need a teacher is that starting out in meditation is like setting out on a journey through unknown territory. We are not familiar with the terrain or aware of the dangers so we need someone who can guide us. A spiritual teacher is a friendly guide, someone who knows the terrain and can point out the pitfalls, tell us which way is to be avoided and which to be followed. The teacher instructs us in the methods we will need to travel the path and above all he introduces us directly to our own true nature. Just as we cannot see our face without a mirror, so without a teacher we cannot recognise the nature of our mind: buddha nature.

Q **Can we meditate without a teacher?**

A Everybody needs a spiritual friend to help them along the path. But if for some reason someone finds themselves in a situation where they have no teacher to turn to, then rather do nothing they should perhaps go ahead and practise meditation - because we have to begin somewhere. But in the long run, and even in the short run, a good friend is helpful and indeed absolutely necessary.

Q **Is there a point, when their meditation practice has developed, when students should leave their teacher and practise on their own?**

A When one has received instruction from one's teacher one must go and practise. However, no matter how far one has travelled on the spiritual path, one should retain a connection with one's teacher or teachers. Otherwise there is a great danger of spiritual pride developing: we might think our progress is due to our own abilities or power. So reliance on the teacher is necessary until the end of the path. In fact, in order to underline this, it is even said that enlightened beings should pay reverence to their preceptors!

In order that we receive the teacher's instructions in the correct spirit it is necessary for us to view him or her with devotion and gratitude. He is the most significant figure in our spiritual life. In a sense he is the representative of the Buddha to us, because he conveys those liberating teachings. If we regard him as base or inferior we will not possess the requisite openness to the teachings nor a sense of their great preciousness. It is for this reason, in other words for our own benefit, that we are advised to generate devotion to the teacher.

It is certainly not the case that the teacher is a saviour. Buddhism is non-theistic, so unlike some theistic traditions, the Buddhist teacher cannot possibly be regarded as a God. To have such an attitude - thinking of oneself as inferior and thinking of a spiritual teacher as a kind of Father god who will pick one up and carry one to heaven - is somewhat infantile and ultimately mistaken. One cannot avoid the fact that though an authentic guru is a necessary facilitator, one must do the hard work oneself.

Q **How do you see your own role as a teacher of a large and ever increasing number of people who wish to follow the Buddha's path?**

A Well, as far as I am concerned everything depends upon my own teacher, Karma Thinley Rinpoche. He made me his substitute and I am sustained in that position by his confidence and his blessing. I am here to pass on to people the things Rinpoche has given me, has entrusted to me. So I know many people come to me for advice and for help and instruction and I try to give it to them, but what I am giving to them does not belong to me. That lineage that I have received from Rinpoche is completely - yes, completely - capable of benefiting all who wish to make a connection with it. So I am allowing people to make a connection - that's how I see it.

Study

Q **How do we study the Buddhist teachings?**

A The first thing we have to be clear about is why we are studying the Buddha's teachings. This is something that very often people in the West are confused about. It is not their fault, it is just that they do not know what dharma teachings are for. What we have to understand from the beginning is that dharma teachings are given so that we can take them away and make them our own. We do this by following a threefold process of hearing, thinking and meditating.

Let us take an example. You might attend a course of instruction being given by a Buddhist teacher. It might be a single session of teaching or a number of sessions. Whichever it is, you would listen carefully to what the teacher says. You would also almost certainly takes notes on what is being said, because that is the only way to remember all the explanations that are given. This is the first stage: the hearing.

The second stage is the thinking. That is when you go away and methodically study what you have learned. That is when you begin to make the teachings your own. It begins to change from being something external that you have heard to something inside of you.

The third and final stage is meditating. This is the stage where you internalise the teachings you have received and reflected on to the point where you can meditate on them. In other words, you are able to use the teachings and put them into practice in your own life.

When courses of instruction are given at Buddhist centres, formal expositions of texts and so on, then being there at the course is just the beginning. That is when you listen and take notes, because you must go away with something to use. Otherwise, being at the course is useless; you might as well go to the zoo or a football match! What is important is that you come away from the teachings with something to work with. You go to the teachings and take notes, then you go away and study the teachings and put them into practice. Hear, think and meditate.

Q How exactly do we go about studying our notes on a particular teaching?

A If it is a particular text you are studying, then you will need to give yourself some routine for study. This of course depends on how much time you have: an hour a day, half an hour or even a quarter of an hour. However long it is, it needs to be something that makes for a regular routine. It is no good spending five hours one day studying a dharma text and then doing nothing for three weeks. The routine, drop by drop, approach is the best. That way you accumulate knowledge and understanding.

Let us say you have half an hour a day. You can first read through your notes on the teaching you are studying, reading only as much as you think you can digest at one time. Then you close your notes and try to teach back to yourself what you have just read. If that has worked, then the next day you begin again. You quickly revise what you have already learned: just a couple of minutes teaching it back to yourself is sufficient. Then you press on with the reading and studying of the next part or point of the text. In this way you are building all the time. You are building your knowledge. By going back each day over what you previously learned you are not losing what you have already studied; at the same time, you are also going further each day.

Through this study process what will happen is that the teaching will start to become a part of us in such a way that it changes our attitude. We start to see the world in accordance with the message of the teaching. If the teaching is about compassion, then compassionate states of mind will arise in us. If it is about impermanence, then we start to sense impermanence and things start to teach impermanence back to us. This is the third stage of the study process, the meditation stage, when the teachings become a living experience.

Studying dharma is not an academic activity. It is a vital practical part of the spiritual path. If we really want to experience the transforming power of the Buddhist teachings, these three things - hearing, thinking and meditating - are absolutely crucial.

Buddhism in the West

Q The archetypal image that Westerners often have of a Buddhist is of a shaven headed monk living in some isolated monastery and it would seem to some people difficult to imagine that Westerners living as lay people with families and jobs can actually practise Buddha's teachings.

A In the Mahayana and Vajrayana Lord Buddha addressed himself to the best way in which lay people could practise the dharma. Of course being a monk or nun is a very valuable thing for many people but it is not the only way to fulfil Buddha's teachings. In the Mahayana and Vajrayana Lord Buddha explicitly declares that buddhahood is achievable by laymen or lay women. In the final analysis, what matters is not our external dress, nor whether we follow the 250 precepts of a monk or the five precepts of the layman or laywoman. What is most important is the depth of our commitment. If our devotion is strong, the essential qualities of compassion and wisdom will arise. In the Vajrayana, the tantric teachings, Lord Buddha set out methods through which laymen and lay women can transform the ordinary experiences of everyday life into the actual means to enlightenment. So for instance the very first time Lord Buddha taught the tantras he gave the *Guhyasamaja Tantra* to Indrabhuti who had asked him for a way in which he, as a layman and a king, could achieve buddhahood. This, I think, is an example of how it is wrong to say lay people can't practise the dharma. It depends on one's character. Some people are more suited to the life of a monk or a nun and I have great respect for these people. They are great examples to those wishing to follow the dharma path. However some people are more suited, through character or circumstance, to the life of a lay practitioner. All are part of the great sangha, the great Buddhist community and this has been especially emphasized in Tibetan Buddhism.

In Tibetan Buddhist history there are many examples of great lay practitioners such as Marpa Lotsawa, the first Tibetan patriarch of the Kagyu tradition. He was a married man who had a family and yet we revere him as the great father of our Kagyu tradition. There is no doubt that he achieved complete enlightenment, as did his wife Dagmema. Also, in the great Sakya tradition Sachen Kunga Nyingpo, the founder father in Tibet, was a layman who transmitted the great dharma of Sakya through his sons and so ensured the continuation of the teachings. There are many such examples and since both Marpa and Sachen had the Mahayana aspiration of achieving buddhahood for the benefit of beings and possessed the great skilful means practices of the Vajrayana, who could possibly question the extent of their realization?

In the West it is now time for study and practice and I hope that in the future we will be able to make monasteries here so that those who have the inner calling to be a monk or a nun can follow the path. For the moment, just as it was in the first hundred to two hundred years in Tibet, it is the time to emphasize study and practice so that the dharma takes root. After that monasteries will grow.

Q **Surely it is much more difficult to practise dharma now in a modern secular society than it was in, say, Tibet in the Middle Ages?**

A Well, I admire - and share - your nostalgia for the past: the eleventh century in Tibet must have been one of the greatest periods for practising dharma. But we can find advantages and disadvantages in every situation. For instance, if you'd lived in a Buddhist monastery in India a thousand years ago, you would have been in danger from the invading Muslim armies. You could have been exterminated in a flash, right there in your monastery!

Coming back to the present, a lot of benefit has come from modern communications. My own teacher, Karma Thinley Rinpoche, lives in Toronto but we can speak on the phone and he can travel to Britain by plane. In other words, modern communications have brought the dharma nearer. The fact that we're actually talking about Buddhism in the United Kingdom is partially due to modern communications.

Generally speaking, however, it seems that there has been a great degeneration of spiritual life because of advanced communications and crowdedness and so on. Therefore I think we specifically need spiritual teachings that are very powerful. The tantric practices of the Vajrayana have the power to turn even negative situations around, because they do not depend on withdrawal from the situation but on embracing and transforming it. So as this dark age progresses these Vajrayana practices will become more and more important.

Q **How do you see the future of Buddhism in the West?**

A When Buddhism was transmitted from India to Tibet it was successful because the Tibetans embraced dharma wholeheartedly. Because they wanted to receive the authentic, pure, uncorrupted dharma, they set themselves the task of receiving all the teachings meticulously from the Indian teachers of the time. So, as the first generation of dharma practitioners in the West we should be sure not to impose our own preconceptions or prejudices on the dharma. It is not the time for us to artificially introduce changes to the dharma.

The dharma will become Western as it takes root in people's hearts. Now it is time to concentrate on the essential dharma teachings through studying them and then fulfilling our understanding through meditation. In this way the teachings will have a firm foundation and the Kagyu, Sakya and Nyingma will have a glorious future in the West.

Q It seems possible that a major difficulty for many people who are interested in Buddhism and who might like to find out more about it and practise it in the way you describe, is being able to distinguish between the many different kinds of Buddhist groups that are appearing in the West. Which groups are genuine, which teachers are genuine representatives of Buddha's teachings?

A Well first of all I think people need to know a little bit more about the history of dharma so they can see which major lineages or dharma traditions have been passed down in an unbroken way to the present day. For instance the Kagyu, Sakya, Nyingma and Gelugpa traditions all offer genuine teachings which have been transmitted in this way. Those who are currently teachers in those traditions are people who have been authenticated by their own gurus and whose gurus were in turn authenticated by their gurus. Thanks to this unbroken transmission of authority, one can go to any of these teachers knowing that one is speaking to a representative of that particular dharma tradition, irrespective of the teacher's renown in terms of the hierarchy. If a teacher is authenticated in this way then the teacher is a genuine master. Those who don't have this authentification are people who have in a sense authenticated themselves as teachers and the wisdom that we get from them will be limited to the wisdom that they possess themselves. However, if we approach and become the student of a teacher of a lineage, it is the wisdom of the lineage that we are inheriting and therefore obviously the best way is to meet those teachers who belong to a genuine lineage of transmission. Therefore we need to know a little about the history and characteristics of a genuine teacher. All these things are spelt out in great detail in the traditional texts such as the *Fifty Verses of Devotion to the Guru* by Asvagosha. As more centres and groups spread here then these things will become part of Western culture, part of the stock of Western knowledge about religion and therefore there will be no room for the spurious, the dubious, the self-appointed.

Q **The community of practitioners which you and Karma Thinley Rinpoche have in this country is known as the Dechen Community. Can you tell us how that community came to be so called?**

A It's had this name for the last couple of years but in a way the community has been building up since the late seventies. However, many of my students repeatedly asked me if we could have a name for the entire community of centres. So finally I asked Rinpoche and Rinpoche told me that he had had a dream the night before in which he composed a spontaneous song. Unfortunately he had forgotten every part of the song except for the line: "the antidote to laziness is great bliss." The word for great bliss in Tibetan is *dechen* and so Rinpoche said that we should call it the Dechen Community. So this is how the name originated. I think it is a very wonderful name, because *Great Bliss* signifies the experience of enlightenment which is the goal of all Buddhist practitioners. It is not a political name, because politics brings great suffering and true religion brings great bliss.

Q **Is it a good idea for us to introduce our children to dharma or should we leave them to find out about it for themselves?**

A From as early as possible one should bring up one's children in such a way that they feel part of the sangha, the community of people following Buddha's teachings. Children cannot approach dharma in the same way as an adult, however, so we need to find ways for them to relate to the teachings. Our generation is the first Western generation to be involved with Buddha's teachings, so it is up to us to find the means to bring our children into dharma. In Tibet, where the culture was wholly Buddhist, children could absorb dharma almost with their mother's milk. That is not possible here. But at the same time we owe it to our children to let them share in what we hold to be the most important thing in our lives. There is no reason for us to feel we have to censor or hide anything about dharma. We should bring our children into dharma and allow them to share in it.

Q **What specific things are there that we can do to bring children into dharma?**

A To begin with, it is a good idea for children to have their own small shrine. This helps them develop a feeling of devotion, a sense of connection, through being able to see a picture or a statue of the Buddha. They can be shown how to make a simple offering such as a flower or a bowl of water. Children, especially younger children, like connective actions of this kind. In addition, they can learn simple prayers and hear and read stories, such as those describing the good deeds performed by the Buddha in his previous lives.

When children get older they are ready to be introduced to the basic teachings. We can explain to them about such things as impermanence and karma, the working of action and result. When they reach adolescence we should encourage them to come to the teachings. Adolescents seem to respond positively to being treated like adults (whether they are or not), so we can use that to encourage them to come to adult dharma events.

Involving our children in dharma is something we all need to work at. Ultimately we would like there to be a Buddhist education for children but that is something that perhaps will have to wait until the next generation.

Q **What should we say to children when they ask us about other religions?**

A If our children come home with other religious ideas they have encountered - maybe a teacher at school talks to them about God, for example - we might say well, that is a very interesting idea but we do not really believe in it ourselves. We can use things like nature to teach our children about rebirth and impermanence and show them that perhaps these ideas about God are a little fairy tale-ish. Of course, if a child has one Buddhist parent and one parent who is, say, Jewish or Christian, then the parents will have to work out between themselves what to say to their child about these things.

The Buddhist Path

Q **Lama Jampa, could you briefly summarize what you feel are the main aims of Buddhist practice?**

A I think the principal aim is to emulate Buddha himself, because Buddha achieved a liberating wisdom which enabled him to work for the benefit of others and the ultimate aim of dharma is to follow his example. Of course many people come to dharma initially in order to solve their own personal difficulties and to achieve personal happiness. However, the final aim is the collapsing of the distinction between self and others and the achievement of buddhahood itself for the sake of all beings.

Q **Many people have the idea that nirvana, the goal of the Buddhist path, is some kind of extinction experience?**

A Who would want to become extinct? Why would anyone waste their time practising in order to become extinct? If they believe in extinction, there are far simpler methods of achieving this. Lord Buddha stated that when we experience enlightenment the fires of delusion, of hatred and of grasping will be blown out and that nirvana is the blowing out of these three defilements. Thus we could say that nirvana is actually the attainment of a naturally existing state of health. Just as a person regains health after being sick, so it is the sickness of self-clinging and all the poisonous emotions that arise from this self-clinging which are extinguished with enlightenment. Furthermore, when they have been extinguished the primordial natural state of wisdom, compassion and great bliss is once more regained, never to be lost again. So in dharma there is a sense of joy because all beings possess within them the seeds of this great blissful enlightenment. So, as we practise, our lives should begin to be influenced and then permeated by this sense of lightness, of joy and increasing confidence in this natural state of health. If a sense of ease and relaxed joyfulness arises in us, it is a sign that our practice is going well. This is not a false joy or a kind of artificial happiness, but a natural unfeigned sense of ease and joy. I think this is a characteristic of Buddhist practitioners and also a characteristic of truly Buddhist cultures.

Q **Would it be possible to say there are distinct levels of Buddhist practice?**

A Buddha recognized that people have different aptitudes, strengths and weaknesses. So rather than reserving dharma teachings for those who come with the deepest motivation, he gave different levels of teaching to suit different people. We can distinguish three levels of Buddhist practice and these levels correspond in a sense to the particular type of motivation and spiritual development of people entering the dharma path.

Q **What exactly are these three levels?**

A These three levels are known as the Hinayana (lesser vehicle), Mahayana (great vehicle), and Vajrayana (diamond or indestructible vehicle). In the Hinayana the emphasis is very much on finding a way to free ourselves from the suffering that we encounter in this cycle of birth and death and from the prison we have built for ourselves through our ignorance. We must then enlarge our vision and develop a vaster motivation - this is the beginning of the Mahayana or second vehicle. In this vehicle the aim is not just our own liberation but that of all beings. Since all beings are interconnected and are said to be 'limbs of one life' it is insufficient to practise only for oneself. Recognition of this places one firmly on the Mahayana path, which is accompanied by a vast compassion and a deeper form of wisdom. One sees not just the insubstantiality of one's personal self but the essential lack of substantiality of all phenomena. The Mahayana in turn gives rise to the Vajrayana, or indestructible, vehicle which is the vehicle that Lord Buddha expounded in the Tantras and which allows those of sufficient spiritual maturity to practise methods which lead to the awakening of buddhahood. This buddhahood is not some external goal to be realized but a buddhahood which is already located within one's own being. Buddha declared that all beings possess buddha nature but do not recognize it because of their ignorance which obscures the true nature of mind. The Vajrayana methods as taught by Buddha are a direct introduction to the totally pure, enlightened nature of mind. The Vajrayana is therefore the highest, most subtle and immediate path of dharma.

Q How does tantric philosophy relate to what the historical Buddha taught?

A We believe that the Buddha taught the Vajrayana or tantric teachings to his most advanced students. Obviously this conflicts with the opinion of some people but I think one can understand it in this way. When a great teacher gives instruction, people in the audience hear it differently according to their backgrounds and aptitudes. Similarly when Buddha taught, those whose principal motivation was to become liberated from suffering themselves heard the so-called Hinayana, those with a vaster and profound outlook heard the Mahayana and those who were ready to recognize the Buddha within and the absolute purity of the phenomenal word heard the Vajrayana. Naturally, because these last teachings were the most sophisticated and difficult to comprehend, at first they had a very restricted audience whereas the Hinayana, being easiest to understand, spread very widely right away and for that reason its followers regard it as the oldest teaching. In fact if one looks carefully even at the discourses of Buddha preserved by the Hinayana schools such as the Theravada, one can see not only elements of Mahayana teaching such as emptiness and compassion but also the basis of Vajrayana, the teaching of the natural purity and luminosity of mind. So although the Hinayanists obviously don't emphasize these things, they are there.

Later on, in the centuries following Buddha's passing, many great practitioners received teachings in visionary experiences directly from enlightened sources. In this way the further elaboration of Tantric teaching occurred. Indeed this process is still continuing in the case of the Revealed Treasures of the Nyingma school.

Q As the highest form of meditation in Buddhism is often said to be mahamudra, could you explain to us what this involves?

A Mahamudra is the meditation transmitted in the Kagyu tradition. In many respects it is identical with the dzog chen teachings of the Nyingmapa school. In mahamudra or dzog chen one abandons the attempt to control or fixate the mind which is characteristic of many systems of meditation but instead allows the mind to settle in a state of natural relaxation. This is like letting the sky become completely free from clouds. When the clouds of agitated thoughts and emotions come to rest by themselves in this unforced relaxation one can recognize buddha-nature, the primordial wisdom that is actually the natural state of awareness. In dzog chen the teacher introduces us to this right at the beginning of our practice and then we stabilize our experience of it through meditation. In mahamudra we achieve stability of mind through meditation and then the teacher introduces us to the natural state of mind. So there is this difference between the two systems but the essential meaning of mahamudra and dzog chen is the same.

Through such practice one realizes that all phenomena are merely the manifestation of mind's energy or luminosity. So there is nothing to reject in whatever appears and also nothing to which one can cling. It is said that "whatever arises liberates itself." Once this is understood we cannot fall back into delusion. So the meaning of mahamudra - 'great seal' - is that everything is sealed, so to speak, with wisdom and the meaning of dzog chen - 'great perfection' - is that everything is perfected in this understanding.

However, we need to approach mahamudra or dzog chen through the various levels of preliminary practice and the skilful Vajrayana techniques known as the *development* and *fulfilment* stages. In that way we create a sure foundation for true realization of these higher meditations. That is how all the great meditators of the lineage have done it.

Money, Drugs & Politics

Q Is there any conflict between becoming wealthy and being a Buddhist?

A Wealth is not the answer to all our problems. It is easy with just a minute's reflection to see that this is so. However, wealth in itself is not bad. It is the unwholesome attitude that fixates upon it that leads to unhappiness. If on the other hand we can view our wealth as a support for a virtuous life and as a tool that we can employ to benefit others, then wealth can be very positive. So if we become wealthy we should recognize this as an opportunity for creative action, not a passport to total happiness nor a burdensome evil.

Q Drug culture was linked to Eastern religions in the 60's.

Do you advocate the use of drugs as an aid to enlightenment?

A Drugs can't really be seen as part of the path to enlightenment. Any apparently spiritual experiences that arise through the use of psychedelic drugs such as L.S.D. and mescaline are experiences that are in a sense borrowed and not a genuine part of one's path. I need hardly say that other types of drugs have nothing remotely spiritual about them. It is true that in the 50's and 60's the use of psychedelic drugs in certain circles did help to create a climate of interest in spirituality and ultimately dharma. You can see this reflected for instance in the work of Allen Ginsberg. However, that time has passed. The dharma is now here in the West and that's all that people need.

Q What is the Buddhist attitude towards politics?

A My own view is that we should walk away from politics. Politics are very powerful and as soon as we start to play the political game, we weaken the power of the dharma teachings. This does not mean to say that we turn our back on sentient beings. What we really want is to have the whole world transformed by dharma teachings - by compassion. But I do not believe that is politics. I believe that is compassion.

Q How do I overcome pain?

A Some of the sorrow that we experience in life is due to temporary agitation and mistaken ideas. As our spiritual practice develops, such trouble subsides. However, there are other forms of pain - mental, emotional and physical - which are more deeply rooted in the human condition. Difficulties caused by others, sicknesses, separations all inevitably occur. When they do, we should see them as the natural consequence of our own actions and not the capricious whim of fate. To see them in this way restores us to a sense of strength, for we have shaped our life and obviously must accept the consequences.

Furthermore, once we have decided to follow a spiritual path difficulties actually provide us with a stimulus to develop patience. After all, how would our capacity to be patient grow if we didn't encounter challenging situations? Finally, the most powerful way to transform experiences of suffering is to utilize them to strengthen our compassionate aspiration for the welfare of others. Just as we may now face a particular difficulty, so many people may be in similar circumstances. Therefore we can generate the wish that these difficulties others face should be absorbed into our own, thus freeing them from their sorrows.

Heart of Gold

T owards the end of his teaching career Lord Buddha is said to have revealed what can be seen as the highest of his teachings. In the period known as the *third turning of the wheel of dharma*, in discourses such as the *Srimaladevi Sutra*, Buddha declared that all beings possess buddha nature. This notion of buddha nature is regarded as extremely important by all the traditions of Buddhism in Tibet.

Buddha nature is the cause of enlightenment. It exists within all beings, like a seed within a husk. If it were not already present in our mindstream, buddhahood would not be possible because it would have to be manufactured. If buddhahood had to be manufactured, it would be contingent upon causes and conditions and would therefore be impermanent. And what would be the use of striving for an enlightenment which did not last?

In reality buddha nature is the true nature of our mind. When we examine mind in meditation we find that it has no dwelling place, no shape or colour and that there is no place where it begins or ends. It is empty of essence. It cannot be equated with what we usually think of as *self*, because there is nothing substantial about it that we can grasp.

Yet although mind is devoid of any substantiality, it cannot be described as non-existent; since all appearances, thoughts, emotions and visions arise from it. This aspect of mind as the ground of all appearances is termed its luminosity: its clear light nature.

We may therefore say that the essence of mind is emptiness but its nature is luminosity. Furthermore, within this empty but luminous mind there is a wondrous, unceasing compassion which impartially embraces all beings. This empty but luminous and compassionate nature of mind is what is meant by Buddha nature.

However, we do not experience this true nature of mind, since it is veiled by emotional disturbances. Owing to lack of mindfulness, our minds have become agitated and this causes us to fabricate the delusion of self and other. This in turn allows emotional disturbances, or defilements, to take hold.

When we have the notion of 'other', we grasp at the desirable other, we hate and reject the fearsome other and we are indifferent towards the neutral other. In other words, the three poisonous defilements of greed, hatred and delusion come into being. These very strong emotional disturbances cause various types of action (karma), which in turn produce the pattern of the world that we come to inhabit: a world characterised by dissatisfaction, insecurity and suffering.

However, throughout this cycle of birth and death the actual nature of mind remains the same - primordially pure - since what obscures it is only the result of delusion. So within samsara, this defiled state of birth and death, dominated by greed, hatred and delusion, there exists the buddha nature which makes enlightenment possible.

But not everyone is able to recognise the buddha nature within. Only those beings who have a precious human life are able to do so. Other types of life, such as that of an animal, a ghost or a hell-being, do not allow the space or freedom to reflect which the recognition of buddha nature requires. Neither does all human life allow this freedom. Human life that is truly precious is not merely the possession of a particular physical structure in which consciousness is embodied but is actually a life in which there are certain moral values and in which dharma is present. Only when human life incorporates these can it be said to be precious, in the sense of its being the working basis of the path to buddhahood.

If buddha nature is the seed, precious human life is the soil. The seed may possess great potential but if it is embodied in the wrong soil it will not come to fruition, until it is transplanted.

We have the seed and we have the soil but the seed needs a careful gardener to water it. The gardener is represented by the teacher. We can understand the role of the teacher in the following way. The journey to enlightenment is unknown to us; we want to set off but we don't know the way. Therefore we need somebody who can guide us along the way.

We might say that we do not need a teacher, that Buddha's teachings are our guide, our teacher. But Lord Buddha gave eighty four thousand teachings, so how can we know which ones are for us? If we merely see Buddhism as a library of possibilities and take bits of various teachings out of it, who is really in charge of our spiritual path? Teaching oneself often means simply confirming oneself in one's own prejudices and never having to encounter anything difficult or painful.

For this reason we need a spiritual teacher. To make the Buddha's teachings effective in our own life situation we need a teacher, a spiritual friend, who will work with us and present and communicate the teachings that are particularly appropriate for us. The teacher is not some kind of saviour who will carry us to enlightenment on his or her wings: he or she is the greatest and kindest of all spiritual friends. In Vajrayana it is said that the teacher is like a mirror showing us our own mind through the transmission of the highest meditation: mahamudra or ati-yoga.

It is the teacher then who endows us with the skilful means, the set of instructions, through which we can achieve buddhahood. This set of instructions has three parts or levels. These are the teachings of the three *vehicles* (yana): the lesser vehicle (Hinayana), the great vehicle (Mahayana) and the tantric vehicle (Vajrayana). All these teachings converge upon a single goal: removing the veils from buddha nature.

One might ask why it is necessary to follow the graduated path of the three vehicles, when teachings such as mahamudra and ati-yoga enable us to recognise and settle in buddha nature immediately.

The reason is that those beings who can benefit from direct transmission without any previous teaching are extremely rare - as rare as stars seen in the daytime.

If we are introduced to the deepest teachings prematurely, there is a possibility that we will misunderstand them and imagine that we have achieved realisation when in fact we have not. Then when we come to see that such realisation is unreal, we will become very jaded with dharma. So although it may be very inspiring to hear the high teachings, we will not truly benefit from them unless we have first obtained a firm grounding in the teachings of the graduated path, such as the four thoughts that turn the mind to dharma.

These four thoughts are the fundamental teachings of the Buddhist path. They are: the preciousness of human life; impermanence; action and result; suffering.

The first thought or contemplation, the preciousness of human life, has already been discussed in detail. This precious human life, however, will not last for ever. Just like everything else, it comes about through causes and conditions: in this case, the union of the consciousness continuum with the sperm and the ovum of our parents. These three elements coming together constitute the basis of precious human life. It is for this reason that the Indian philosopher Nagarjuna was able to say:

"Life is as fragile as a bubble on a stream:
After breathing out,
It is a miracle that we breathe in again;
On going to sleep,
It is a miracle that we wake up."

This is the second of the four thoughts that turn our mind to dharma, the contemplation of impermanence and death. The teaching on impermanence and death is the greatest stimulus to action and sweeps away much of the rubbish with which we fill our lives: the material, political and emotional goals in pursuit of which we fill our days. As the famous Tibetan yogin Milarepa said: "It was thinking of impermanence that made me go and meditate."

When we are very young we think that everything will be the same forever, that we can turn to dharma later. But contemplating impermanence makes us realise that the time to turn to dharma is now and that, if we are to do this, we must clear away everything that is not essential. In the words of the bodhisattva of wisdom, Manjusri, who appeared to the Sakya master Sachen Kunga Nyingpo: "If you cling to the things of this life, you are not a dharma person." The way to stop clinging to the things of this life is to take impermanence seriously.

The third thing we need to think about is karma: action and result, cause and effect. This will enable us to distinguish between those actions we should undertake and those we should avoid. Every common sense person knows that if you plant a certain type of seed you get only a certain type of fruit. Similarly, if we act positively we benefit ourselves and others for the future; while if we act negatively we poison ourselves and others for the future.

The view of the highest meditation, the ati-yoga and mahamudra, transcends limited notions of good and evil; but if we think that because we are meditators moral behaviour is not important, we are mistaken. Only a Buddha is perfectly good. In the Nyingma tradition of Buddhism, it is said that one should have a view as vast as the sky and actions as scrupulous as an atom. If we do not apply this in our own behaviour, the deeper teachings will not work. Lord Buddha taught three trainings: first morality, second meditation and third wisdom. To claim to follow Buddha's teachings but to take exception to parts of them is like going to a doctor for advice and then not taking the medicine he gives us because we do not like it.

The fourth and final thought that turns the mind to dharma is suffering. We understand something about suffering through the contemplation of impermanence. However, to understand Buddha's teaching on suffering properly, we must realise that suffering does not come about just from a temporary life situation but is the result of the iron grip of ego. Because of this, suffering is built into experience in all the realms of samsara, the cycle of birth and death, from the highest heaven to the deepest hell. Even when there is great love and joy between people, ego intrudes, manipulating the experience, turning the other person into an object, the relationship into suffering.

These four contemplations, the four thoughts that turn the mind to dharma, are the fundamental teachings of the Buddhist path. If we take them to heart and contemplate them, in sitting meditation and in everyday life, then we will definitely have entered the dharma path and the deep teachings of the second vehicle, the Mahayana, will become relevant to us.

The chief characteristic of the Mahayana is compassion: a compassion which resolves to embrace the suffering of others and which is produced by dedicating oneself to bringing about the benefit of others.

As the basic dharma teachings loosen the grip of self-cherishing and self-importance, we start to become open to the existence and needs of others. We begin to extend the same care and attention to their experiences as we do to our own. This openness radiates outwards in love and then compassion. Love is the wish that everybody may have happiness and the causes of happiness; compassion is the wish that these beings may be free from suffering and the causes of suffering. Meditation on these two things, love and compassion, was taught by Buddha as a catalyst for the thought of enlightenment (bodhicitta), which is the resolve to become enlightened for the sake of others.

So after the four thoughts, we should meditate on love and compassion. There are many methods of doing this. The Tibetan tradition takes the attitude that we should start with a specific person, usually our mother, and then learn to bring everyone else into the clear focus of our meditation. Our mother is usually chosen because she is the person with whom we have the strongest link in this life and to whom we have the biggest debt, in terms of what we owe her for her unselfish kindness and compassion towards us. In this way our meditation retains a strength and an intensity that would not be there if we began by thinking about loving everybody in general.

Through this sequence of love and compassion in both formal meditation and everyday life, we come to realise that the needs of others are as great as our own. In fact their needs are greater, because there is only one I while there are countless others. If we truly want other beings to have happiness and freedom from suffering, we must be able to bring this about. And the only way to do this is by calling on our own inner resource by becoming a Buddha.

This recognition is symbolised in the bodhisattva vow ceremony. In the ceremony, we say in the presence of our teacher: "I will become a Buddha for the sake of others, just as the Buddhas of the past have done." When that intention awakens in us, we are really in the Mahayana, the great vehicle.

Now that we have entered the Mahayana, how do we fulfil this resolve to become a Buddha? It is said that there are two ways. One is to put into practice the six perfections of the bodhisattva path: giving, morality, patience, energy, meditation and wisdom. The other is to enter into the Vajrayana, the third vehicle.

The Vajrayana path provides the most rapid route to enlightenment, because it possesses so many skilful means and practices. Moreover, in the Vajrayana there is no need to practise asceticism or to turn away from sense objects, since these are seen as primordially pure.

So if we develop the Mahayana attitude of love and compassion, which is itself based on the proceeding Hinayana teachings of the four thoughts that turn the mind to dharma, and if we have the good fortune to meet Vajrayana teachers who can give us initiations and instructions, we should enter the Vajrayana - but only with the aim of becoming a Buddha for the sake of others. This last point is very important, because sometimes in the West, people believe that Vajrayana is an alternative to Mahayana and Hinayana, when it is in fact the culmination of these two. The Vajrayana teachings will not work unless we have accomplished the preliminary teachings first.

Each of the four main traditions of Tibetan Buddhism cherishes particular lineages of Vajrayana. The Gelugpa tradition, for instance, specialises in the Guhyasamaja and Kalachakra tantras. The Sakyapa tradition focuses on the tantra of Hevajra and, based on this, the famous meditation teaching of *The Path and Its Fruit*. The Kagyu tradition specialises in the meditation of mahamudra; the Nyingma tradition in ati-yoga, the direct path which, like mahamudra, strips away all obscurations from the purity of primordial mind.

The fruit or culmination of the spiritual path is buddhahood. Yet buddha nature is pure and perfect as it is and has not been improved by the path. Buddha nature is like gold within ore. When the ore is taken away the gold is seen as it is. It cannot become any purer, since it was totally pure already in itself. Similarly with buddha nature, even though it is surrounded by the veil of defilements, it is already primordially pure. When the teachings cause the veils to disperse, this is buddhahood and buddhahood is no different from the basis, which is buddha nature.

When we practise meditation we can easily be misled into thinking that our efforts will produce buddhahood. If this were true, buddhahood would be a conditioned reality and as such would be impermanent. The language of dharma urges us to accumulate merit and gather wisdom which will lead to buddhahood but this is only a skilful manner of speaking. The teachings do not actually do anything to our buddha nature at all: they simply remove the veils that obscure it from our vision.

Thus it can be said that the only difference between a sentient being and a Buddha is that a sentient being is someone who has not recognised the nature of mind and a Buddha is someone who has.

Buddhahood is not an extinction but continuing activity for the sake of all beings, When the veils surrounding buddha nature are removed, it is like a lamp being released from a pot. If the pot is smashed, the lamp lights up the whole room. Similarly, when the veils are removed from buddha nature, buddha activity irradiates the whole world with endless compassion. In the *Uttaratantra Shastra*, Maitreya says that buddha activity is unceasing non-conceptual activity for the benefit of others.

Glossary

Ati - yoga
The highest teaching of the Nyingma tradition, also known as *dzog chen*. According to this teaching, the fundamental basis of the whole of reality is the primordial awareness itself inherent in all beings. This basic ground is empty, luminous and compassionate. Since all phenomena manifest from this foundation, they are all intrinsically perfect. Since everything is therefore perfect as it is, buddhahood is attained without the need for acceptance or rejection.

Bodhicitta
The wish to attain buddhahood for the benefit of all beings and the application of this resolve through spiritual practice. Ultimately, bodhicitta is insight into the emptiness of all phenomena.

Bodhisattva
A being in whom bodhicitta has arisen and who has thus dedicated himself or herself to achieving buddhahood in order to bring about the temporary and final well-being of all.

Buddha
The principal of enlightenment; an enlightened being. In particular, Shakyamuni Buddha, the 'sage of the Shakya clan' who taught the way to enlightenment in India 2,500 years ago.

Buddhahood
The state of enlightenment attained by the bodhisattva, combining recognition of the true nature of mind with continuing compassionate activity for the sake of all beings.

Buddha nature
The true nature of our mind, which is empty and luminous. When the veils of ignorance that envelop our buddha nature are cleared away, this is buddhahood.

Dharma

The Buddha's teaching.

Dzog chen

See *Ati-yoga*.

Gelug

The tradition of Buddhism founded in Tibet by the scholar Tsongkhapa (1367 - 1419 CE). The chief characteristics of the school are its emphasis on monasticism and its adherence to Tsongkhapa's interpretation of Mahayana philosophy.

Hinayana

The first of the three yanas or levels of spiritual practice in Buddhism. Hinayana practice emphasises the contemplation of fundamental Buddhist teachings such as impermanence and suffering, leading to renunciation and realisation of the lack of any personal self.

Kagyu

The tradition of Buddhism established in Tibet by the translator Marpa (1012 - 97) and his spiritual heirs Milarepa (1040 - 1128) and Gampopa (1079 - 1153). The principal teaching of the Kagyu school is mahamudra, the meditative realisation transmitted to Marpa by the tantric masters of India.

Karma

Buddha taught that all our actions of body, voice and mind inevitably have consequences, for good or for bad. Our present situation is the result of our previous actions; what we choose to do now will determine our future experience.

Mahamudra

In the Kagyu school mahamudra is the meditative accomplishment through which one directly settles in and recognises the nature of mind.

Mahayana

The second of the three yanas or levels of spiritual practice in Buddhism. Mahayana practice stresses the compassionate motivation of bodhicitta and the wisdom of emptiness.

Nirvana

The cessation of ignorance, greed and hatred and, in consequence, freedom from inevitable rebirth in samsara. The goal of the Hinayana path.

Nyingma

The oldest tradition of Tibetan Buddhism, originating from the teachings of the eighth century Indian masters Guru Padmasambhava and Shantirakshita. The principal teaching of the Nyingma tradition is ati-yoga.

Sakya

The tradition of Buddhism established in Tibet by Konchog Gyalpo and his spiritual successors, the Five Masters of Sakya. The tradition takes its name from the monastery founded in 1073 by Konchog Gyalpo in the Sakya area of Tibet. Its principal teaching is *The Path and Its Fruit*, the meditation system originally transmitted by the ninth century Indian yogin Virupa.

Samsara

The cycle of birth and death, whose characteristic is suffering and whose origin is unawareness.

Sangha

The 'community' of people, lay and monastic, who are following the Buddha's teachings. The 'noble sangha' is the assembly of those who have attained spiritual realisation through practising the teachings.

Shastra

A philosophical treatise or commentary on Buddha's teachings.

Sutra

The discourses of the Buddha, in which he expounded the teachings of the Lesser and Great Vehicles (Hinayana and Mahayana).

Tantra

The 'continuum' of the inherent wisdom-mind that is present in both ordinary beings and enlightened beings and which makes possible the experience of enlightenment. The tantras are the esoteric teachings of the Diamond Vehicle (Vajrayana) given by Lord Buddha.

Vajrayana

The third and final level of Buddhist practice, expounded by Buddha in the tantras and providing especially powerful methods for spiritual realisation.

Yana

The vehicle that carries the practitioner along the path to enlightenment. Generally the Indo-Tibetan tradition of Buddhism identifies three main spiritual vehicles or levels of practice: the Hinayana, Mahayana and Vajrayana.